In the Mind's Eye

Art Shimamura

Copyright © 2017 by Arthur Shimamura.

All rights reserved. No part of this book may be reproduced in any form or by any electronic or mechanical means, including information storage and retrieval systems, without permission in writing from the publisher.

Broken Memories

Kelp I

Kelp II

Anthurium

Papaya

Rose

Calla Curves

Leaf Abstract

Tree Lane

Reeds

Autumn Leaves

Gracefully Aging

Aging Iris

Aging Curl

Aging Tulip

Cormorants

Olympic Spring

Badlands

Yosemite Storm

Pt. Lobos Rocks

Wood Abstract

Stream Leaves

Mt. Lassen Snow

San Francisco I

San Francisco II

Metropolis

New York Jazz

Academia, NYU

Bodie

Tate Modern

Pont Royale, Paris

Utah Salt Flats

Bristlecone Pine

Lanikai

Leaf Drops

Maui Trees

Barbers Pt, Oahu

Sunset Beach, Oahu

Big Island Reflections

In the Mind's Eye

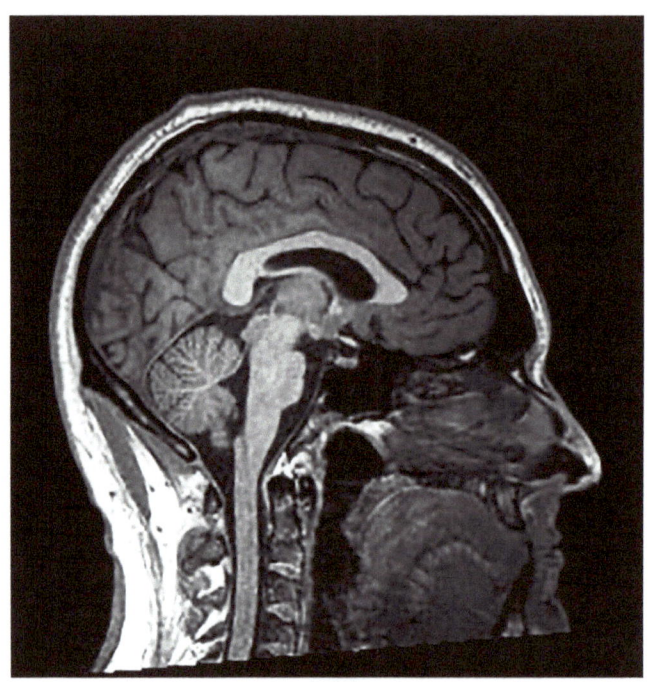

Thinking of you...

—Art Shimamura

www.ingramcontent.com/pod-product-compliance
Lightning Source LLC
Chambersburg PA
CBHW051103180526
45172CB00002B/757